The Big in the World

by Joy Cowley
illustrated by Diane Perham

LEARNING
MEDIA®

Mrs. Delicious got a truck full of flour for the biggest cake in the world.

Mrs. Delicious got a tank full of milk for the biggest cake in the world.

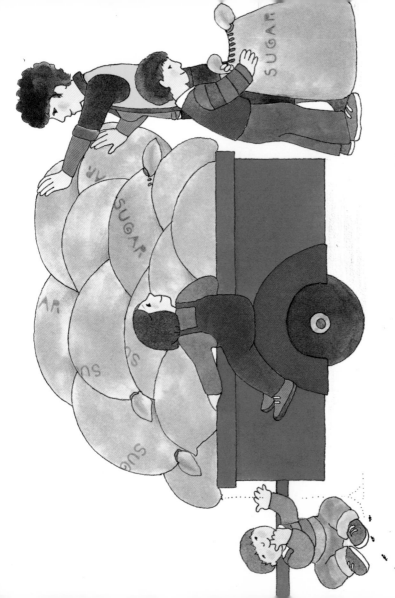

Mrs. Delicious got a load of sugar
for the biggest cake in the world.

4

Mrs. Delicious got a thousand eggs
for the biggest cake in the world.

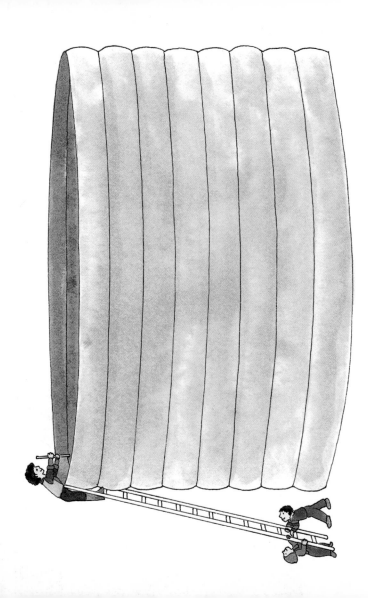

Mrs. Delicious mixed and mixed the biggest cake in the world.

6

Mrs. Delicious cooked and cooked
the biggest cake in the world.

Mrs. Delicious got a tractor to pull the biggest cake in the world.

Mrs. Delicious got a chain-saw to cut the biggest cake in the world.

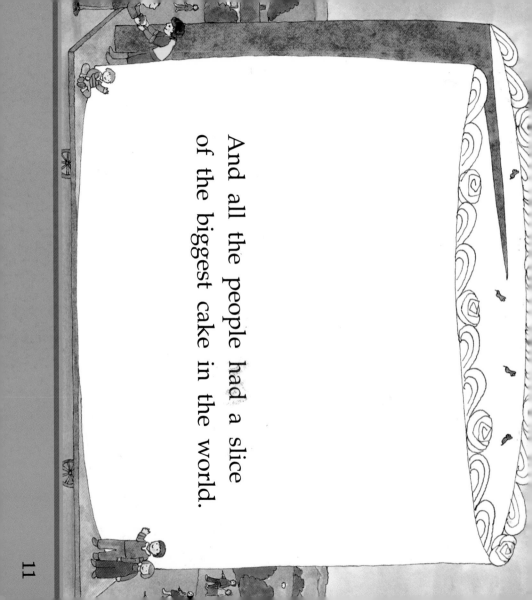

And all the people had a slice
of the biggest cake in the world.